THE
GRACE BETWEEN

THE
GRACE BETWEEN

D. John Maclennan

Regent College Publishing
www.regentpublishing.com

The Grace Between
Copyright © 2015 John Maclennan

All rights reserved. No part of this publication may be reproduced, stored in a retrieval system, or transmitted, in any form or by any means, electronic, mechanical, photocopying, recording or otherwise, without the prior written permission of the author, except in the case of brief quotations embodied in critical articles and reviews.

Published 2015 by Regent College Publishing

Regent College Publishing
5800 University Boulevard, Vancouver, BC V6T 2E4 Canada
Web: www.regentpublishing.com
E-mail: info@regentpublishing.com

Regent College Publishing is an imprint of the Regent Bookstore <www.regentbookstore.com>. Views expressed in works published by Regent College Publishing are those of the author and do not necessarily represent the official position of Regent College <www.regent-college.edu>.

ISBN 978-1-57383-523-7

Cataloguing in Publication information is on file at Library and Archives Canada.

CONTENTS

	Foreword *by James Houston*	7
I	Night	11
II	Journeying	29
III	Understanding	47
IV	Fortitude	65
V	Hymns	83

foreword

Speaking as a poet, W. H. Auden observed that reading great literary works "read us" more than we can "read them." In communicating his own feelings, the poet expresses our own personal sensibilities. John Maclennan does this, freeing us to disclose ourselves, hopefully, gratefully, yet domestically, in the ordinariness of daily living. It is humility and simplicity which speak a universal and humane language. It is autobiography at its best, when it transcends the facts of the 'bio', to give insights into the processes of the soul.

The apostle Paul reminds us we are but "cracked, earthenware jars," which yet contain the prospects of the glory of God (2 Cor. 4:7). As one commentator has observed, John's collection of poems resemble *Kintsugi*, the Japanese method of repairing cracked pottery by infusing gold into the cracks. Glory replaces weakness. It is the opposite of what is an old practice in the dinghy light of Near Eastern bazaars, of filling wax coloured appropriately to hide the cracks and appear to be *sine cera*—without wax. But sincerity is a questionable virtue. Divine grace is best.

The five sections of John's poems—Night, Journeying, Understanding, Fortitude, and Hymns—can be interpreted autobiographically, or they can be viewed as daily pulse beats of every day.

foreword

The family DNA of John is full of enterprise, travel, diverse creativity, and wide-ranging relationships, expressive of all the suffering of the twentieth century. John's poems are expressive of all this: living on four continents; trained in physics; an only child who was interned with his parents by the Japanese in eastern China, where his grandfather as a Scots engineer had first helped to build roads; his father later worked with the British trading firm Jardine Matheson. At school in Hong Kong and later in Sydney, Australia, John completed his education at Edinburgh University with B.Sc. and M.A. degrees.

He later embraced the life of Norway, with its sheer beauty of mountains and fiords, and since 1997, he has also embraced like splendour in British Columbia, making his final home in Vancouver. But with each embrace it is friendships that motivated each move.

Why then begin an anthology of poems with 'night'? It is because depression of spirit and darkness of soul form a continuum for every human being, seeking God. John needed Prozac and prayer, not as one symptom needing relief, but as living as an embodied person, with both body and soul. Thus in one poem, John conjoins both as "the lies of yesteryear come back to haunt us / and tell us we have lost our life." So in the night, "I pray to Christ to rescue us / from every surrounding snare and pit."

The 'Night' then propels John to start 'Journeying': "I will take a lead / From where you lead me... until I see / The light that's dawning." It is a search for 'Meaning', for "words are just words," but what God says "is what you mean. Show us the way to your meaning...." So this may

foreword

mean leaving behind "yesterday's friends / Waiting by the roadside / With nothing to say." But "a new way forward" is that which leads "upward to everlasting life." So we urge others, as "we talk to your soul / not to your face."

Relationally, John now finds he cannot communicate with those who "use words that don't mean what they say / words that are twisted and bent." But then he finds the same about himself, "Do I understand myself?" Mutually, 'Party Time' is just "chatter and talk." But in seeking to know God, "I don't understand why you forgive me." Now John can exclaim: "I think I have found the answer / To what I set out to seek / The treasure in earthen vessels / That makes us weep and weep and weep."

'Fortitude' now becomes a new friend for John, now propelled forward by the desire for the Eternal:

> I wish I were there
> I wish I were already there
> Meeting with Jesus
> Meeting with God

But meantime, we too, with John, can sing hymns. For "I love the Lord with all my heart / And I will serve him all my days." All of life can now be rehearsed once more, but with joy in our hearts, to interpret it all so differently. Come, as we "forget ourselves / And serve you, / Until you come again." John, perhaps as a George Herbert of our day, invites us, as his readers, to join joyously in the pilgrimage to Mount Zion.

We don't speak great truths, we live them simply. This is what John's poems demonstrate.

I
Night

My Picture

A woman dances in vibrant red
Her hand lifted, cleaving the air
Every movement expresses emotion
But her face has an air of despair

Behind her the audience watches
Serious and wrapped in their thoughts
Gazing steadfastly onwards
Awaiting an answer to prayer

What can I say of this picture
Studied by the guitar player there
Can it answer my questions that question
The meaning of hope in the air

Longing

The roar of traffic racing by
Helps us to remember
Our priceless lives
keeping pace with it

Stop cars! and listen to my haunting cry
I wake the dead who hear me
Past rapidly roll their years
And endlessly return

To suffer and to sigh
And wish
That they had never been

Expression

Positive is peace like a river
Running to and fro
Whispered lightly along the ground
Told to Everyone round

Everyone knows what happens tomorrow
Everyone Understands
I don't

A Poem of Despair

I saw the mirror in the glass
And all the vibrating surrounding life
I could have forgot it if I tried
But gazed on it and lost my life

How easily said, how easily done
We don't remember what we said
The lies of yesteryear come back to haunt us
And tell us we have lost our life

I do not wish to think on that
But to blot it out is far too hard
The knife into the wound is set
And will not come out without a life

I pray to Christ to rescue us
From every surrounding snare and pit
So that the Devil will not boast
That he has led us down to it

Anger

I forgot you when you began speaking
Don't do it again.
My Anger wells up like a fountain
Don't do it again

Explosive things happen today
Things that have no end
Do you remember them?
I will never forget them

Shame

It is the twilight of my soul
When wrath and anger struggle here
It is the ending of my name
When I must bear the brunt of blame

I wish it could be otherwise
I wish that time could be reversed
So broken dreams could be restored
And all that was could be renewed

It cannot be, I must await
Whatever time and God decree
I must bow down before my fate
And bear the fruit of iniquity

A Painful Memory

Was it yesterday the world stood still?
Or was it the day before
It began to fall apart?

I would like to remember
The time before that happened
Yet it is too painful to forget.

Endless yesterdays unrolled before then
Endless tomorrows came afterwards
Help me to remember the time when....
Help me to forget.

The Worries of Life

Sundays come rarely
Heavy days hover round us
There is no escape
There can be no peace

The burdens we carry
The burdens we bear
The worries we walk with
Our lives filled with care

Enjoy life while it is now
The pressure of time will sweep it away
Ended forever
Remembered no more

Memory

Shadows play quietly upon my wall,
They upend themselves with upside-down motion,
I will never know where they come from,
They whisper tales of long ago.

Ashes and Dust! Ashes and Dust!
Report their histories which tell of tomorrow
And round the balance wheel goes
Asserting their stories.

They drag up mirror images of the hidden past
They sweep onward with never-ceasing pace
Until they have called from the depths
All that can be remembered.

St. Columba's Isle

Oh beige brown spots on green hillocks,
Tussocks of emerald grass
Oh ruined piles of ancient stones
Where once bishops pontificated.

Oh that you could see a revolution in your state.
That life might once more through you course
Decisions be made and live people talk.

But you are only ruins,
Ruins of a bygone state
Edges without a body
Night beyond the gate.

The Moving Chain

A restless consequence of moving chains bites the dust,
Sonorously it roars on,
A rumbling ever moving weight
Cascading inconsequentialities out of its mouth
As tho' there were no tomorrows.

Fleetingly it skims the water of change
Monotonously it etches figures out of nothing
Harbour and docks are near
And rest consummates the unending motion.

Illness

The Sea Caspian washes all around me,
Breaking me into bits.
But I will join together in a oneness
Of triumphant light.

I am being tested in the furnace of tension
I am being savagely sawed and shaped,
Twisted and turned and moulded,
But I will come forth triumphant.

For a little while I am being bitterly baked,
For a little while I am a creature,
A caricature of myself.
Tossed and tormented, winnowed and stripped,
That I may prove your triumphant will.

Soon all will be over,
All will be at peace,
And I look forward to the harbour moorings
Of the quiet haven
Where I will be at peace.

Descent

Aphrodite in a cupboard
Bare and polished, honed and dry
We could make our life on airships
We could make them fly.

Twelve noon strikes the note of doom
Each stroke resonates so firmly
Each stroke hammers on the tomb.

Life is vacant, life is empty
Fitted for eternal note
Constancy in seeing plenty
And being savaged by a quote.

Epithalamion of tears
Turgid river play of words
Softly, softly cross my heart
Whisper words that echo fears.

When will you be finished time?
When will you be all wound up?
Glimmeringly you spoke in rhyme
And held forth the dreaded cup.

When the Snow Came

When the snow came it was a quiet
World of distance and stare
All the world disappeared
Into a redundancy of white ash

Burning, burning, burning
The constancy of Sin
Forgiveness like water poured
On an open wound

Welcome light
A dawn-filled rhapsody
Of overwhelming light
Please continue to come
And end the sorrow of night

Sorrow Over Lost Time

You told me you loved me yesterday
But I did not understand
Yesterday gives way to tomorrow
And I have nothing in my hand.

Some people are steadfast and true
Others wane with the telling
What they said
Is lost and gone
And what they thought
Returns to their sorrow.

I know now that I will never learn
All that life means and says
My yesterdays vanish unmentioned
And my tomorrows never see day.

Despair and Hope

In bleak despair I stared about
Winter only comes but twice
It winds its fangs about my throat
And gurglingly applies the final twist

We will be home with you
In a better place
Where leaves fall pleadingly to the ground

I will remember this dream
And come back to it over and over again
It is the promise of a bright tomorrow

II

Journeying

Journeying

I will take a lead
From where you lead me
Over hill and mountain shore

Until I see
The light that's dawning
Ever more, for ever more

This is bittersweet to taste
When I taste it day by day
Show me nightly where it's leading
And the place that I will stay

Roads run onward into Heaven
Where I'll come to rest at last
Lead me safely ever onwards
Till I reach the Home that's just.

The Search for Meaning

I saw a sight upon a hill
burnished green and red
I thought I never would it find
But You came down instead

Lostl The key to afterlife
Lost! The way ahead
I will find it if I seek
Roses green and red

A Poem About Nothing

What does it matter what happens tomorrow?
The world turns and twists
Frantically weaving
A garment of truth for a world full of shit.

Yesterday I discovered the truth
Now I no longer know what it means.
What I found was a kernel of nothing
Emptying the world of its truth and its bliss.

I darkened the world with a suicide's aim
And ended its pretensions to truth
I stripped off its robe
And looked underneath
And found nothing there but a twisted up mess.

Tell me the Truth Lord
To a worlding's ravings
Empty my search for all the wrong things
Show me what it means
To Know You and Love You
And find there the meaning to All This.

The Old Soldier's Song

I woke and called it yesterday
As trumpets brayed retreat
I heard the sound of battle songs
And knew it was defeat

Fire over fire had rained on us
And shook the very earth
We tasted blood and sweat and tears
And came to a new birth

Advance! they cried
And urged us on
Retreat our souls would say
Life's very essence poured out
At the dawning of the day

Goodbye to battle sounds and storms
Goodbye to fiery dread
We walk on earth a chosen race
Who bled and bled and bled

And now I come to peaceful times
When the battle reigns no more
To armchair ease and cups of tea
And steps behind the door

Thoughts

April showers come daily
Clouding the day
Love comes rarely
Having nothing to say

I wish I knew the future
How the days would unfold
Life's rhythm changing
Happiness untold

Answer me Gods of War
Talk to me Gods of Peace
I am waiting to know you
To feel your release

Heaven

Ipse Dixit said the man
Who poured out the tea
And waved to heaven
On his way there

It's time to forget
When first we went there.
Time to remember
Another time
When the flowers bloomed

And all the fruit was in season.
It was a time dug out of the past
Blessed and Holy
Not to be forgotten

But to be treasured.
I will try to remember it
And dwell on it
And come to it again

Nature Talking

Fish in the sea
Turning and Turning
Talking to each other
While the water's churning

Speak to me fish
Of the time that is past
What you remember
Buried in Dust

Then it was morning
Rising again
When the world spun
And welcomed the sun

Now it is evening
With a promise of night
Your words I must hear
Ere God puts out the light.

Silence

The epitome of your meaning is silence
We pore over the words
And reach an astonishing conclusion.

Words are just words
And what you say is what you mean.
Show us the way to your meaning
Write it out in a painful scrawl.

Then we will believe it
Then we will know it
All in all

Telling Your Friends

I came upon yesterday's friends
Waiting by the roadside
With nothing to say.

I will speak to them words that I know
I will show them the way to speak
They will open their mouths and say
Every word that I teach

Passing Time

Yesterday, Yesterday, Yesterday
They keep endlessly coming and going
Do they tell me anything I want to know?
They keep coming forever

I have found the speech they speak
Nothing but rubbish and gabble
Bury it deep in the aeons of time
So that they will never come near.

Buying a Car

So much done
And I have forgotten none of it.
It reaches into the interior of my mind
And empties me of sense.

What have I learnt from this?
That the world begins turning tomorrow?
I really do not know.
I can make no sense of it.

Life itself is there
Full of the unexpected
We cannot understand it
We should not even try to.

Echoes

What were you doing, when I called to you,
Calling upstairs
Echoes calling back and answering
It went on all my days.

I was discovering something as I went along
Something to remember and recall
In later times

That was a discovery
That went on into a future time
Echoing and calling back
To the time that is now.

Reflections on the Reality of Worldly Things

The world turns around us, puzzling and glaring
Its essence of Reality is not revealed
In the disturbance of the mind

Who can fathom it? Who can know
How it twists and turns and forms itself
Into something akin to slavery

Reality is a strange thing
Not easily understood
It hides itself behind a changing show
So that it is impossible to reach

About Fish and Chips
(Working Class Complaint)

Fish and chips on Sunday
Fish and chips on Monday
When will time's timeless grinding end?

I work hard all day
And sweat and toil
Doing something for nothing
Or nothing for something
And it's all just a bad smell.

But you reward me with fish and chips
I should slap your face with the fish
And cram the chips down your throat
But I don't.

I eat them up calmly
Thinking how awful life can be.

Upward and Onward

What did we understand from all this?
What we never understood before,
That life turns around us
A circle in space
Beside an unending shore.

What it said, it told us
Clearly and free
And we must accept it
And learn where it goes.
A trickle that's nothing
Swelling into something.

Something that teaches us day after day
What we need to learn
And where we should go.

Now we have learnt it
Now we know
That the future around us is just a show
And we have a duty, a way to go
That leads upward and onward
Where, we will never know.

The Way Forward

A field of leaves
A field of green
How is life caught betwixt and between?

But I have found on the path of sorrow and dread
That the dead never listen or raise their heads.

But I have found freedom
A new way forward
Where paths of life commingle and meet.
Such a path should always be taken
It leads forward and upward to everlasting life.

The Message

Evermore I see you
Before my face
Evermore I tell you
To leave the race

I trust you will listen
And hear what I say
I talk to your soul
And not to your face

The time is coming
When I will talk no more
Hear me and listen
Ere I talk no more

III

Understanding

What You Meant

What were you doing when I talked to you
Trying to guess the implications of what you meant
You were difficult to understand

Your talking goes on and on
Touching the edges of time.
It dulls my thoughts
Like a broken stick
Yet speaking of you

Say no more that will not last
But handle the truth carefully
It shines a light on my path
So that I understand

Self-Doubt

I thought I understood you
What you did and what you meant.
Now I know I don't
And that ends our chat

You use words that don't mean what they say
Words that are twisted and bent
And point to an end
That never returns
Which I can never find out.

Do I even understand myself?
Made up of mysteries, lost, yet existing
Riddles and words turning
Round in my head
That I in the end must spit out

Party Talk

I visited someone and
They had nothing to say
I told them everything
From the beginning of the Day

Tonight we celebrate
To a party we go
To chatter and talk
About all that we know

Talk and talk endlessly
From beginning to end
Till each other
Away we send

A Speech

You spoke about yesterday before it came
And twined it into a cup
That tasted like poison

Open our ears to hear your voice
Sugar coated and anonymous

Covering our ears
I will remember tomorrow
When tomorrow comes
And confuse all that you said
Into a myriad yesterdays

The Way

Impossibly at odds with the world
I stood and stared at its unfolding nonsense
Where will I learn?
When will I know?

God told me there would come a time
When all my schemes would be unravelled
I'm waiting for it.

Come, time that God knows,
Come and enlighten me
Show me the way

God's Forgiveness

You told me what was happening
But I didn't believe you
Now I reap the consequences
For ever

Thank you for being so explicit
And not sparing me
I will never know why
You have forgiven me.

How to Understand

Things happened today which I don't understand
I met no one I knew
And heard no strange things.

It seems life goes on as before
Rippling and turning
And showing its face of care.

This means we have come to the bottom of things
Deep in the river, where?
It still makes no sense to my silly old mind
And tells me nothing I did not know before.

More Life

What have I found through life
What have I discovered
That it is an endlessly repeating song
Where nothing ever comes back ever

I liked it while it was going on
I found I had a way to go
But its rewards were bitter illusion
Which slowed and slowed and slowed.

I think I have found the answer
To what I set out to seek
The treasure in earthen vessels
That makes us weep and weep and weep.

It is to be patiently accepting
Of all that life unfolds
To mix the bitter with the happy
And to know it will never be told.

Afterwards (3)

When something is done that cannot be undone
What then? – afterwards
I wallow in remorse
And destroy the memory –
but it still remains.

I have refused to confront the past before
But it always wins
Triumphing over me and breaking my heart.

Suddenly there is a new day
And morning comes
Lighting the Dawn
And filling all the world with light.

I know what I have learnt from this
And it is understood
We draw a line under the past
And forget it.

A Poem to Young Faces

How shall the old greet the young?
Whispering across the years
How can we meet and understand
The changes that our lives steer.

These questions defy understanding
Riddles that are open, and show
No one has found the answer
Or found a place to go.

Why do I bother to ask them?
Questions that don't have an answer
I think I'm understanding something
Something I will finally know.

A Life of Flowers

There was dew on the grass last night
And flowers swayed in sympathy
Today will unlock their thoughts
That reveal the passage of time

I have understood it all
Their growth ---- a symphony
Where one flower speaks to another
And they all enjoy the time.

Found

After daybreak the night fell.
Lost in a ditch
We found you.

Afterwards we came to ourselves
And wondered where you'd been
But it was Grace that found you

I saw your eyes
Like twinkle toes looking behind you.
Where had you come from
Where were you going to
Only God knows

Understanding You

When will the world turn again
And stop to speak to me?
I have so many things to say
All the words of all the Day

Thank you for endless listening
Thank you for breaking my heart
I will write your words down carefully
And keep them far apart

I thought that I learned and knew you
Through all the days that have passed
Now I think I understand you
At last! At last! At last

Finding Understanding

The war was fought to bitter defeat
Even before it began
I can never understand, nor ever understood
Its ever changing plan.

But please don't teach me
Morning after morning,
Of how it changes and goes
It never made sense to me and never will
Unless I'm ultimately known.

I have found an answer
Deep in my mind
Which satisfies me to know
It is not the answer I hoped to find
But its meaning will plainly be shown.

Wasted Time

Ah, useful time
Well spent on things,
Dreaming and Scheming,
And rushing around

I wish I were there
Back in the present
Pushing all else behind me

The beautiful future
Opening its gates
Bidding me welcome again

I'll shut it all down
Say no to its gifts
And turn my back on it all.

What Life Means

Dear friend I see you
As You pass by
Saying hello to your friends
And wishing them well

Say Hello to me
On your journey through life
So that we may know
What it means

Enlightenment

I saw you coming through the dark
And all your way was shown
And then I knew the answer was
All that I had known

It wasn't easy finding it
The Way was long and hard
But what you said was shown to me
Until I knew your word

It could be a lightning stalk
That flashed upon my way
But knowledge is an eerie thing
And who am I to say

IV

Fortitude

The Shadow of the Past

The squeezed out rags of yesterdays
The haunting past of lost innocence
Will we ever be whole again

God enters with his masterstroke
He who dwells in the heavens forgives
All the past is washed away

And there is a new beginning

The End

The Appropriateness of life
When will it end?
Going on and on
Spinning into eternity

I wish I were there
I wish I were already there
Meeting with Jesus
Meeting with God

Age

One year follows another
The years pile up
Echoing from one to another
Preaching undying songs

What can you teach me, years?
What can you tell me, life?
Read me the story of man
Whisper his tale of strife

Out of your womb comes learning
Out of your rest comes joy
As we tread the steps of our lifetime
As we walk in the vale destroyed

We long for the morning ascendant
We long for the rise of the Son
When all that is past will be over
When all that is ended, begun

The Effect of Time

The dark days slip away
Into an endless night
How does one day pass
Slipping from sight

Would that they came back to us
Shining and new
Showing us everything we wanted to do

But time passes onward
Relentless and slow
Ending our dreams
And destroying our hope.

But light shines from the heaven
Resplendent and bright
And destroys all the shadows and darkness of night
Till we come to a place where we see and believe
That what was lost we can now retrieve

The Future Opening Up

The gate to the future is open
We have only to wander in
And find what it means to be lonely
And know the journey of sin

It's a path that frightens and scares us
A pathway of fear and dread
God receive us please, I beg you
So that no more may be said

You are a God who rescues
Forward and back through the years
You are a God who saves us
Ending a life full of tears

Knowing God

I was seen before I was born
Known before I came to be
Oh God who determined my destiny
Where were you when I called?

That time of hardship I endured
bitterness fighting against hatred
All the way.

You were the terminator
You enriched my life with flowers
You gave me hope

Fortitude

I will bear the blows of fortune
I will take what heaven sends
I will wend my way thro life
Till I reach the end of ends

Tomorrow will rise sunblest
All those yesterdays forgot
What has been will be no more
What was then and what was not

I will stride the path of hope
Till at last it leads me home
I will know the fortune finished
Time at last to cease to roam

That will be a day of glory
That will be a day of hope
That will end my endless story
That will break the final rope

Going Home

Today I saw the sunset
I heard its whispered voice
I love it for its colours
I bless it for its choice

I will not always look on it
I will not often hear it tell
Of time that has been past
Of roads I know so well

Those yesterdays are now forgot
Those pathways are now trod
A new way dawns before me
A new way home to God.

Hearing from God

I saw you come from heaven's gate
Your arms outspread to greet me
Your word was mine to meditate
And I will ever see you

Thank you Lord for all you've done
To smooth my path before me
To open ways I would not have known
And give me ways to heal me

From this time forth
I'll know your voice
And know you're ever near me
So speak Lord, loud and clear
So I will ever hear you

Faith

Astrophysics is an important science,
It wraps up the stars in an infinity of words.
But you are my deliverer O God,
Hidden but not lost, hunted for but not found.

In the endless wrapping of eternity
Who will unravel the eternal mystery?
Who will declare it before the face of the people
And absolve them from their guilt?

You are the Lord, the Eternal One,
You will unravel the Secret
You will loose the knot
And all time is in your hands.

Bewhiskered we go down to death,
It meets us with open arms,
But see, here comes one greater than death
Here comes the deliverer.

Happiness

Happiness comes
Stolen from yesterday
Illuminating the sun
And leading the way

Thank you for its joy
And all the peace it brings
Wavering without annoy
And filling what has been

Sometimes it goes
And leaves me alone
Playing with things
That have never been

But it will come back again
Time after time
Until I am satisfied
Tasting its joy

A Christian Poem (2)

Lord of our life
We lay all before you
Work on us!
Transform us into images of glory
Don't forget us.

Crooked is the path that leads
Past many briers and hedges
You are the one who leads us
And brings us home

Show us your eternal kingdom!
Vanquish us with your strength
Swallow us eternally
That we may know you
And love you

Happiness (3)

Happiness is a twice told story
Told in Age and told in youth
An endlessly circulating myth
Which refreshes and retells itself
Through the Ages

But misery comes,
And with its sharp contrast
Fills our soul,
And alters our point of view

But time turns endless
And happiness returns
Visiting us with new vistas
Wrapping us in endless tomorrows

Heaven and Earth

I saw heaven opened
And a land of glorious light
From which Evil had disappeared
And Hell had taken flight

Christ and God in council stood
Within that vast domain
And nothing could be heard
But the angels' swelling strain

They praised them for their majesty
Their glory and their might
They threw themselves before them
And they worshiped day and night

Can we on earth
Hear a faint echo of that sound
And know our future is bound up
In all that comes around?

Yes, indeed we can
And know for certain
What it means
The glory that awaits in the land that has always been.

Answer to Prayer

It took me by surprise
When you spoke
The times that were past
The times yet to come

It was all unwrapped
Revealed in an instant
About how it would end

I was amazed
Dumbfounded
At the answer given
Thank you.

Towards the Light

My dreams of yesterday come flocking back
All you taught me, all I ever knew
It was a curtain lifted on the world before
Disturbing, haunting, pointing to a distant shore

Now I know the meaning
That you tried to show
Now I feel the way before me clear
And it doesn't disturb me while I go

The past comes back to haunt me still
But the future lies open clear and bright
And now I know the way to go
The way that leads me to a land of light

V
Hymns

God's Way

All glory to God in the highest
Who reigns here on earth today
You have opened the gate to heaven
Along the narrow way.

Thank you for being our saviour
Thank you for being our friend
What on earth can we give you
For the endless treasures you send

I know at last your meaning
I can see at last the light
The things I once thought I knew
Have vanished into the night.

Receive from us your praises
Doubled and redoubled again
For everything that you have done for us
For all the things you made plain

Praise

Thank you for all you have given
Thank you for all you have made
Worlds without end unrolling
Evermore singing your praise

Forever we beckon and raise you
Forever we sing and enjoy
The worlds you have laid out before us
Which all of our songs employ.

You were there when we hadn't existed
You are there for evermore
God, we sing your praise forever
Till you finally shut our door

A Poem to You

You came to me out of the darkness
And filled my world with light
You came to reassure me
And blot out forever the night

Thank You for being my Leader
Thank You for being my Guide
For all the ways You teach me
And that You stand by my side

I will always praise You
Forever as days go by
What you say lifts my heart to greet you
So that I know what is a lie

Give me the whisper of morning
Show me the way that is true
So that I will know the meaning
Of all that l have to do.

God's Beauty

The beauty of a flower
Mirrors the beauty of a tree
The beauty of its face
Mirrors that of you and me

All nature conspires
In a resonating chorus
To mirror God's beauty and grace
And all of the facets it shows
Reflect from his wonderful face

It was ever thus so
From the beginning of time
And will continue for ever so
As long as his breath upholds
Everything in its place

A Prayer to the Eternal

Lord you hold the earth in the span of your fingers
All the earth is afraid of You
Destiny is in your hands
To all the ends of the earth

I will praise You in majesty
And kneel in fear
Hold out your hand to raise me up
Your love to shape me

Oh the wonder of your greatness
Forgotten yet always remembered
Breathe life in your creation
And death to your foes

Forever I will love You
And call on You for help
Do your will for me
And fasten up my life

A Love Poem

I love the Lord with all my heart
And I will serve him all my days
When times of difficulty come
I'll find him in the Way of ways

He is our teacher and our friend
Our leader and beloved guide
With what he knows He leads us here
And shows us the sure safe way to take

What a Son and what a God
Their love is endless and deep
And leads us out of darkness here
To the land where they appear

There we'll know them as they are
And stand in awe of all we see
And feel the peace that comes from them
And know at last that we are free

Being Sick

I saw the flowers dancing in an endless stream
I saw the world turning as an endless sphere
I loved you Lord before time began
I'll rest in you for evermore

You spoke of Freedom
You spoke of Hope
You told me not to give in
I know you'll receive me tomorrow

An angel spoke
Clouds danced before my eyes
It was a glorious sight
Hallelujah for evermore!

Thank You, God

How beautiful is the world You made
Scintillating and dancing in the sun.
The flowers declare Your majesty
Even those things lurking in the shade.

Your mercy shines bright
On the least of your creatures
On the way You have carved for them
They hasten and grow.

Even we whom You made
To talk to You
Are shaped and prepared
For the way we must go.

One day we will thank You
For all You have done for us
Kneel and adore You
The Giver of Grace
Who has blessed and kept us
To worship and know You
And to find in You at last the place we will go.

God Cares for Us

Afterwards I understood
What I never knew before
That as You speak your will
We discover the way before us clear

Thank you for being our father
Caring for us as if we were sons
Showing the way that is leading
To life within your dear Son

All these things we know
And they all give glory to You
Our father and carer forever
Until at last we be with You

Happiness

Thank you Lord for all you send
Your gifts of everlasting end
Birds and flowers that squeak and grow
Ways that end in endless snow

We happy ones who know your grace
We know we'll see you face to face
Send us days of light and hope
Endlessly our ending break

Gifts of bread and love and wine
Reach us from your endless sky
Turning all our days to grace
Till we see you face to face

God's Truth

The Truth of your word is eternal
Lasting while worlds come and go
Your message rings out forever
It tells us more than we know

Can we pretend to weigh it or understand it
To fathom its mystery sublime
Such thoughts show our limited reasoning
That echoes and changes with time

Thank you for being our father
Thank you for being our friend
The truth that we know is eternal
That will go with us on to the end.

The Battle of Life

The sea comes in, the sea goes out
Reflecting all our life about
When will its changing ever cease?
And lead at last to our release?

I saw it come; I saw it go
A changeless and unending show
It taught me there was no way out
No end to tears of woe and doubt.

You are the God who leads me out
Who breaks its cycle with a shout.
You lift the curtain on its end
And lead us where You would us send.

Thank You God, for all You've done
Thank You for the Way You've won
It is a way that leads to life
And puts an end to hopeless strife.

A Long Journey

God, you are the beginning
God, you are the end
All the ways that you lead
All the ways that you send

Come to my heart
I implore you
As onward and upward I go

My Life is the journey unending
Along the Way without light
You open the way before me
Leading me on through the night

Thank you for being my Saviour
Fighting my battles for me
Releasing your power to aid me
Finally bringing me life

God's Peace

You gave me the peace that I feel
All that I've known forever
You give a gift that is real
A gift you will never sever

Thank you for being my friend
As aeons come and go
Helping me on to the end
With all that I know I know

You will stand with me at the Gate
And show me the way that goes in
It's never, never too late
To blot out the shadow of sin

Blessings upon you forever
We say from first to last
We have understood the way to glory
And tasted the final repast

Thanksgiving

Oh God who made the spheres
In multitudes around us
And bade the world stand still
Upon the day you found us

You chased away our fears
And on us shone your blessings
You swept away our tears
And called to us from heaven

We love you and adore you
And endlessly surrender
Our loves and hopes and fears
Unto your endless glory

As time goes by
We love you
We worship and adore you
Forget ourselves
And serve you,
Until you come again

About D. John Maclennan

John Maclennan has lived on four continents and travelled extensively. His poems are the result of an active yet reflective life.

Both of John's parents were adventurous people, each pursuing their own career in China when they met. John's mother, Christina Morrison, pursued her nursing career in Shanghai at the Country Hospital while his father, Donald, worked with the British trading firm Jardine Matheson.

Not long after John was born in Hong Kong, his family moved back to Shanghai and were living there when World War II began. The Japanese eventually took total possession of Eastern China, and John and his parents were interned from 1942 to 1945 at an agriculture academy in the countryside. Each family lived in a single room, and their food was limited to rice and a few vegetables. The adults worked on the land during the day, and the Japanese guards patrolled during the night. By the time the war ended, they emerged much thinner, but alive. Looking back, John felt they were fortunate to be located in a rural area rather than a city.

After the war, John travelled with his parents back to Scotland aboard the British troopship "Oxfordshire." However, once he had settled his family in safety, Donald returned to Hong Kong to continue his business career. In 1947, he again brought his wife and eleven-year old son out to join him. John attended school in Hong Kong until he was sixteen.

After finishing high school in Sydney, Australia, John completed his education at the University of Edinburgh, receiving both a Bachelor of Science and a Master of Arts degree. He was subsequently employed by the Institution of Electrical Engineering in Stevenage, near London. He coded abstracts, wrote indices for articles, and occasionally wrote abstracts when needed.

John moved to Norway in 1981. He loved this country; being a very compassionate man, he appreciated the high quality of life for all citizens. He learned Norwegian and settled happily into life there. However, when John's mother's health began to fail, he returned to Edinburgh to look after his parents during their final years.

There, he met a remarkable Anglican rector and began attending Roger Simpson's church. It was at this time that John became more interested in Christianity and began a program of philanthropy.

After living in Norway again for 2 years, John decided to follow his friends the Simpsons and moved to Vancouver in 1997. Here John has continued his pursuits, developing a steady discipline of writing poetry.